Addison-Wesley Mathematics

Assessment Handbook

Guidelines and Suggestions for the Classroom Teacher

Addison-Wesley Publishing Company

Menlo Park, California ▪ Reading, Massachusetts ▪ New York
Don Mills, Ontario ▪ Wokingham, England ▪ Amsterdam ▪ Bonn
Sydney ▪ Singapore ▪ Tokyo ▪ Madrid ▪ San Juan ▪ Paris
Seoul ▪ Milan ▪ Mexico City ▪ Taipei

Contents

ISBN 0-201-86672-2
2 3 4 5 6 7 8 9 10 ML 98 97 96 95 94

Introduction

The **Addison-Wesley Mathematics Program** is designed to help teachers meet their assessment requirements. It offers the busy teacher ways to verify that students are learning to be effective problem solvers who can apply skills and concepts of mathematics. *Addison-Wesley Mathematics* assessment provides:

- information that lets teachers make meaningful instructional decisions
- feedback to students to let them know how they have progressed
- information for parents and administrators regarding the success of their children
- experiences for other tests mandated by schools, districts, or state agencies

Addison-Wesley Mathematics assessment materials are practical to implement, appropriate for the students' developmental level, and instructive in their own right. Because no single approach can provide a complete picture of what students understand, assessment in the program ranges from informal suggestions in lessons to several kinds of formal tests. These tests reflect both the *Addison-Wesley Mathematics Program* and standardized tests. Included are:

- objective multiple-choice and free-response tests
- performance-based assessment materials

There are also self-assessment opportunities, including the use of portfolios and math journals.

Overview of Assessment Options

Here are the assessment tools you have available in *Addison-Wesley Mathematics*. In the chapter management pages of the Teacher's Edition you will find more detailed information including page references to your Teacher's Edition and Student Edition.

Informal Assessment

- Ongoing **Observations and Informal Assessment** in the Teacher's Edition for each core lesson.
- **Observation Checklists** to record thinking and cooperative learning actions, in the Record Keeping Forms booklets.

Traditional Testing

- **Quick Quizzes** in the Teacher's Edition for each core lesson.
- **Mid-Chapter Reviews, Chapter Review/Tests,** and chapter **Cumulative Reviews** in the Student Edition.
- **Free-Response** and **Multiple-Choice Tests,** for each chapter and for mid-year and end-of-year testing, which can be tracked in Record Keeping Forms or in the Computer Management System.

Alternative Assessment

- **Performance Assessment** for each chapter in the Student Edition.
- **Performance Assessment** and **Alternative Assessment** booklets with assessment activities for each chapter.
- **Portfolio Assessment** support in this booklet and in the Teacher's Edition.
- **Student Math Journal** suggestions for self-assessment.

Effective Assessment

Traditional Assessment: Skills and Knowledge

Traditional tests usually include multiple-choice and free-response tests, and are often very focused on the skills and knowledge that the student has been learning, as shown by these examples.

A Divide: $45 \div 8$.

B Write and graph an inequality for the statement "Price x is more than \$5."

C Draw the next shape that continues the pattern.

 ___

The Student Edition provides mid-chapter reviews, chapter review/tests, and cumulative reviews. The Teacher's Edition provides Quick Reviews, Quick Quizzes, and Item Analysis charts.

There are also separate **Free-Response Tests** and **Multiple-Choice Tests** for all grades. These booklets include Mid-Year and End-of-Year multiple-choice tests. The chapter tests provide four test items for each cluster of core objectives, as indicated in every chapter's management pages in the Teacher's Editions.

The Mid-Year Test is a forty-item test and covers the essentials of the first half of the year. The End-of-Year Test is eighty items long. The first half covers the same material as the Mid-Year Test.

The results of these tests can be kept in several ways as indicated in the management section on page 13 of this booklet.

Assessing Problem Solving and Communication Skills

Thinking, problem solving, and communicating are vital skills, and current trends in assessment are beginning to reflect that growing emphasis. To meet those needs there are Performance Assessment materials in the Student Edition, and separate Alternative and Performance Assessment Chapter Tests, as well as suggestions for portfolios, math journals, and self-assessment, which are discussed in the remainder of this booklet.

Performance Assessment

Performance assessment includes a variety of methods: some paper-and-pencil tests, projects, and manipulative experiences provide other opportunities for performance assessment.

Common features are:

- **The work or activity that the student performs is authentic.**
  Here is an authentic problem for an adult: "Given your income and budget, how much can you afford to spend for a new car, taking into account the cost of the car, gas, repairs, insurance, and tolls?" There is no easy approach; there is a need to gather data, including a lot of estimated information; there is usually no clear-cut answer; and when you do form an answer, it is subject to change. Student versions would often have open-ended situations in which there may be no clear answer or multiple possibilities.
- **The work is often varied in methods used and in the way results are presented.**
  Students may be given a problem such as: "Find the typical height of students in your classroom. Prepare a graph or graphs of heights that shows how heights vary in your class." Results could be given as a stem-and-leaf graph, bar graph, box plot, or data table. It could even be a cleverly arranged group photo.
- **The student usually needs to display communication skills.**
  Questions often include the requirement that students justify their work. It is appropriate to consider how well the student presents information. If, however, a student displays understanding and obtains good answers, that should weigh more than how results are communicated. ESL students, for example, should not be penalized for a lack of command of English.
- **Evaluation of the work is often multidimensional.**
  Performance assessment usually indicates a more complex task than is found on ordinary tests. It is useful to have established criteria (a scoring rubric) by which the students' work is evaluated. More is said about this in the next three pages.

Performance Assessment Samples

Here is a sample problem, with three responses.

> Mike is planning a bike trip from home to the beach, a distance of 54.8 km, according to a friend. The trip involves crossing a small mountain range about 600 m high, so Mike thinks he will be able to travel at about 19 km per hour to the beach and 16 km per hour on the return. He plans to stay at the beach about 1 hour. He wants to get back home by 5 p.m.
>
> Schedule Mike's trip. Suggest a good time for Mike to start, and explain your reasoning. Drawing a picture may help.

Joline's answer

The trip is sort of a long line, like this:

home — beach — home again

54.8 km	1 h	54.8 km
19 kph		16 kph
54.8/19 = 2.88 h		54.8/16 = 3.42 h

total = 2.9 + 1 + 3.4 = 7.3 h

7.3 h = 7 h (3/10) x 60 min or 7 h 18 minutes.

Mike should start about 7 or 7½ hours before 5 p.m, between 9:30 and 10 a.m.

Barney's answer

Mike's average speed is (16 + 19)/2 or 17.5 kph. He wants to go 109.6 km. So divide 109.6 by 17.5 to get 6.2 hours. One more hour at the beach gives 7.2 hours or 7 hours and 12 minutes. So, Mike should leave home at 9:48 a.m.

Miles' answer

Mike should leave in the morning, because he has to cross a hill and will get tired.

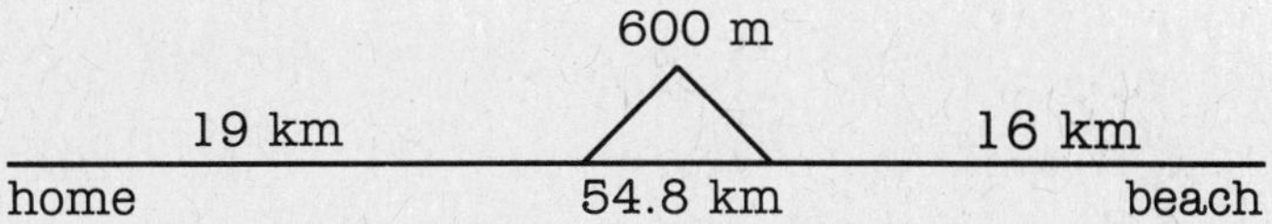

Evaluating Performances: Rubrics

Evaluating a student's performance entails looking at the work from several views and making distinctions more refined than simply identifying right or wrong answers. A rubric, which is just a guideline for evaluating students' work, can help to assure a consistent "grading" approach.

The rubric suggested in *Addison-Wesley Mathematics* has four levels. This is recommended for a combination of ease and a reasonable amount of discrimination on tests used to determine how well a student has done at the chapter level. For each problem students are given a score of 4, 3, 2, or 1.*

The basic structure is as follows:

4. Full accomplishment
The student applies appropriate mathematical skills, concepts, and techniques; communicates the results using appropriate means (writing, diagrams, graphs, non-paper-and-pencil media); and justifies or explains her results as appropriate to the task.

3. Substantial accomplishment
The student uses appropriate mathematics, but may make a few simple errors in computation, or similar mistakes. Student indicates an understanding of the appropriate mathematical concepts. Communication is fair, but could be stronger, clearer, or more complete.

2. Partial accomplishment
The student gives an incomplete and possibly erroneous response, misapplying the mathematics. May show that the student has a misconception or limited grasp of the mathematics. Does not address the conditions of the situation, may use poor reasoning. Results are inadequately reported.

1. Little or no progress toward accomplishment
The student does not deal with the central mathematical idea or does not try.

* In commercial or state-prepared performance assessment instruments , a 5-, 6-, or 7-point scale is often used with each test item to make sharper discriminations, but these are typically used annually, not with the frequency of chapter tests.

Performance Assessment: Sample Evaluations

Let's review the sample responses in terms of this rubric.

4. The student uses the relevant data, creates a model as a diagram, description, or set of equations, computes the answer using concepts of distance, time, and speed, and reports results with meaningful precision.
3. The student completes the problem, but may not communicate clearly, or may not apply appropriate concepts completely. Communication is adequate.
2. The student misuses or fails to use mathematical concepts. Modeling is inappropriate. Communication is inadequate.
1. The student does not deal with the central idea or does not try.

Joline's answer

Joline would probably get a 4. The sketch is an effective model. The math is correct. The precision is rough, which is appropriate for the problem. She is not distracted by the irrelevant information.

Barney's answer

Barney mistakenly averages the speeds. It gets him a value between 16 and 19 kph, which is near the true average, so his work will be close. Still, it is a misconception. He is not distracted by irrelevant data. He is overly precise in his answer. He should probably get a 3.

Miles' answer

Miles creates an unworkable model. His response is only weakly appropriate and would not provide the biker any service. Miles probably should get a 2.

Performance Assessment Preparation and Follow-Up

We all like to know how we are to be evaluated, so discuss with students how you are going to evaluate their performances **before** they start. You might conduct some assessments as group activities. And, after their performance and your evaluation, you might use them as the basis of a wrap-up discussion. Students can share ideas and approaches.

Portfolios

A portfolio is a sampling of a student's work selected over a period of time, such as a semester or a year. It gives a picture of the quality of a student's work, and of the growth and change in a student's mathematical capabilities.

What Belongs in a Portfolio

The contents of a portfolio usually meet criteria such as these:

- **The work should be significant and interesting.**
  This will vary greatly among students. For some it means the results of a complex project. For others it may mean a simple assignment completed perfectly for the first time.
- **The student should want it in the portfolio.**
  The portfolio represents, among other things, what the student thinks represents her.
- **The portfolio should cover as long a time span as possible.**
  This assures that the portfolio can show growth and change in the student's mathematics capabilities.
- **The portfolio should contain from six to ten entries.**
  A difference between a cumulative folder and a portfolio is the selection process. A portfolio includes thoughtfully selected entries chosen to satisfy the requirements listed above.

Suggestions for entries are given in the management pages of the Teacher's Edition. These often include small projects or work on data analysis or problem solving done in cooperative learning groups. You and the school may also determine that portfolios should include test results or other items.

Who Selects the Entries

The choice of people who select depends on how the portfolios are to be used. The student normally selects the entries with the teacher's guidance and approval. The school may also require specific contents.

Documenting an Entry

When an entry is chosen by the student, she should describe it and indicate why it was selected. This self-assessment practice will assure that students' choices are made thoughtfully and deliberately. A teacher or aide can interview younger students and fill out the form. The student should also maintain a portfolio Table of Contents so that a viewer can readily scan the scope of the portfolio. The next two pages show a Portfolio Entry form and a Table of Contents form to be used as prototypes.

Evaluating Portfolios

Portfolios have been evaluated by students, teachers, parents, committees of teachers, school officials, and state groups. The criteria for evaluation depend upon who is evaluating and for what purpose. Often, portfolios assessed as a group, such as a whole school or district, help to evaluate the effectiveness of a program.

Portfolios evaluated by students and parents help them both to understand the students' progress.

Your evaluations give you further perspective into how your class is progressing, as well as a chance to reflect on your own program.

Other Portfolio Suggestions

Portfolios can be quite diverse, reflect the personality of the student, and be a focus of pride and accomplishment. Consider the following:

- A poster done for a combined art and math project.
- A set of graphs done as a data analysis project, done with a computer.
- A report on a mathematical or math-related topic.
- A photograph of a project, or a set-up of manipulatives made by a student to demonstrate a math concept.

There is opportunity for fun, the display of accomplishment and excellence, and sharing of new and exciting ideas!

Portfolio Entry Form

Name ______________________________

Date ______________________________

Give a title to your entry ______________________________

Describe your entry in a sentence or two.

____

____

____

____

____

Tell why you want this work in your portfolio.

____

____

____

____

Math Portfolio Table of Contents

Entry	Date	Title
1	________	____________________
2	________	____________________
3	________	____________________
4	________	____________________
5	________	____________________
6	________	____________________
7	________	____________________
8	________	____________________
9	________	____________________
10	________	____________________
11	________	____________________
12	________	____________________

Self-Assessment

Self-assessment is based on the idea that a student's perception of her ability and accomplishments is significant.

Informal Opportunities

One way to have a student assess herself is to pose a question in the course of a lesson or work session.

- *Marie, when you solved the problem, how did you check to see if your answer was reasonable?*
- *Roberto, how did you use those counters to show place value?*

Student Journals

Having students write in a journal is a way to help them internalize what they are learning. You can have the students write (or draw) entries on a daily basis. One way is to give them the start of a sentence and have them complete it.

Today we learned that . . .
I was surprised to find out that . . .
The toughest problem I solved was . . .
Here is my graph of . . .
I'm not sure how to . . .
This is my example of a function: . . .

Teaching Aid

Math Journal

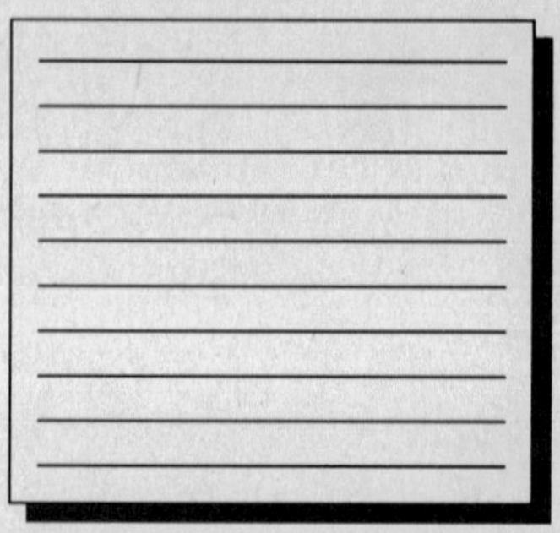

Blackline masters of journal pages are in the Teacher's Support Package.

Keeping a journal helps to develop communication skills. Usually a student has to describe a process, procedure, concept, or object; recording such things is a needed skill in many professions that comes from practice and experience. Sketches, diagrams, charts, and graphs are forms of communication and should be encouraged.

Portfolios and Self-Assessment

A significant opportunity for self-assessment is a shared review of a student's portfolio. As the school year progresses, you and your student can examine the progress of her work and you can discuss how she is growing and changing.

Managing Assessment

The *Addison-Wesley Mathematics Program* has a collection of management information and tools that can help the teacher plan coursework, track progress, record information, and evaluate progress.

The **Teacher's Edition** is the fundamental management tool. It contains program, grade level, chapter level, and lesson level views of the work, the amount of time to devote to a chapter, and activity and assessment options. It deserves study, and will become a friend with new ideas year after year. The chapter management pages will provide you with a picture of the objective clusters and portfolio opportunities. The lesson notes will give you meaningful informal assessment suggestions.

The **Record Keeping Forms** will assist you in recording the progress of students who are using the Free-Response and Multiple-Choice Tests. It also provides cooperative learning and complex thinking observation checklists to aid the teacher in recording students' behaviors.

The **Cumulative Record Book** will assist the school in recording the progress of a student as she works through the entire program from grade K to grade 8.

The **Computer Management System** records the progress of students on Free-Response Test and Multiple-Choice Tests. It also provides summary reports of progress of the individual student and the class, and reports for the students' families.

Record-keeping support is also provided as an integral part of the **Performance Assessment** (grades 1 and 2) and **Alternative Assessment** (grades K and 3-8) **Teacher's Edition Booklets.**

References

Assessment is one of the hot issues of the 1990s. As this booklet shows, there are many aspects to assessment and evaluation, and there is a broad span of literature that can be useful to the practicing teacher. Listed here are some references that are insightful, contemporary in their outlook, and worthy of a busy teacher's time.

Hart, Diane, *Authentic Assessment: A Handbook for Educators,* Menlo Park, CA, Addison-Wesley Publishing Company, 1994. An effective classroom tool for the elementary and high-school teacher in any academic subject.

Freedman, Robin Lee Harris, *Open-ended Questioning, A Handbook for Educators,* Menlo Park, CA, Addison-Wesley Publishing Company, 1994. Guides teachers who wish to write and use open-ended questions, develop evaluation rubrics, and evaluate student responses, in diverse subject areas.

Webb, Norman L., ed., *Assessment in the Mathematics Classroom, 1993 Yearbook,* Reston, VA National Council of Teachers of Mathematics, 1993. Very practical and focused for the school mathematics classroom, with further bibliographical references.

Curriculum and Evaluation Standards for School Mathematics, Reston, VA National Council of Teachers of Mathematics, 1989. The "Standards" that are guiding much of the current change in school mathematics education in the 1990's.

Brandt, Ronald S., ed., *Readings from Educational Leadership: Performance Assessment,* Alexandria, VA: Association for Supervision and Curriculum Development, 1992. This is a collection of over thirty articles on performance assessment.

Romberg, Thomas A., ed., *Mathematics Assessment and Evaluation: Imperatives for Mathematics Educators,* Albany, NY: State University of New York Press, 1992. Discusses aspects of and trends in external assessment, such as state-mandated tests.